The Old-Fashioned CONGRATULATIONS POSTCARD BOOK

A Sterling\Main Street Book

Sterling Publishing Co., Inc. New York

10 9 8 7 6 5 4 3 2 1

A Sterling/Main Street Book

Copyright © 1993 by Sterling Publishing
Published by Sterling Publishing Company, Inc.
387 Park Avenue South, New York, N.Y. 10016
Distributed in Canada by Sterling Publishing
% Canadian Manda Group, P.O. Box 920, Station U
Toronto, Ontario, Canada M8Z 5P9
Distributed in Great Britain and Europe by Cassell PLC
Villiers House, 41/47 Strand, London WC2N 5JE, England
Distributed in Australia by Capricorn Link Ltd.
P.O. Box 665, Lane Cove, NSW 2066

Manufactured in Hong Kong
All rights reserved

ISBN 0-8069-8770-7

The occasions for offering congratulations to family and friends are as numerous as the fruits of good fortune or hard work—a new job, a new house, a new child, a business promotion, a scholarship or fellowship, graduation, a winning lottery ticket. In short, we offer congratulations to those who succeed, to those who get out of life what they want. Though nothing may succeed like success, as the old proverb goes, good luck runs a close second. Either, when enjoyed by the people we love or like, will claim our joyful participation through a hearty offer of congratulation.

The practice of writing to friends and relations to wish them well on happy occasions warranting congratulations is as ancient as the art of writing itself, but the sending of preprinted greeting cards to extend such wishes is a relatively recent tradition. The first commercial congratulations cards, in fact, date from the early twentieth century, during the height of the picture postcard craze. All the congratulations cards reprinted in this book originally appeared between 1907 and 1914, the years between the Federal Government's decision to permit handwritten messages to appear on the address side of a penny postcard and the decline of the postcard industry after the introduction of greeting cards with envelopes. At the zenith of the picture postcard's popularity (1913), Americans bought some 968 million cards.

The golden age of postcard art comes alive in *The Old-Fashioned Congratulations Postcard Book*. Each card, printed in its original vibrant colors on heavy mailing stock, is perforated for easy removal. And each card provides ample space on the reverse side for the sender's personal wishes. At a cost of less than 25c each, these period postcards are not only a greeting card bargain, but an imaginative and tasteful example of the cardmaker's art suitable for the most deserving recipient.

Most of the postcards in this book were supplied by Don and Newly Preziosi, dealers in vintage postcards and paper. Information about their holdings in a large number of postcard collecting categories can be had by writing Preziosi Postcards, Box 498, Mendham, New Jersey 07945.

Heartiest Congratulations

HEARTIEST CONGRATULATIONS

Congratulations

Congratulations

From *The Old-Fashioned Congratulations Postcard Book* © by Sterling Publishing Co., Inc.

Congratulations

HEARTIEST CONGRATULATIONS

S-104

HEARTIEST
CONGRATULATIONS

341-D

Heartiest Congratulations

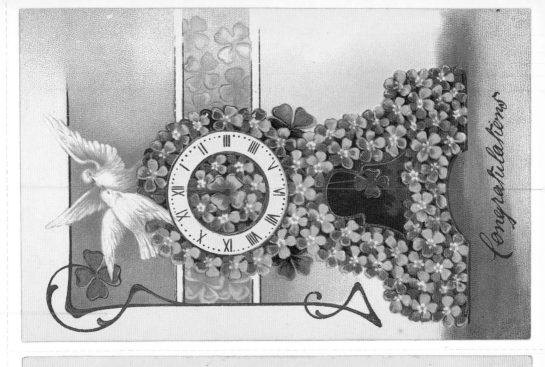

Congratulations

Congratulations

Congratulations

1048.

Heartiest Congratulations

Heartiest Congratulations

Congratulations

Heartiest Congratulations

Heartiest Congratulations

Will you let me be
your noble cavalier?

Then I'll give you posies
every day this year

Hearty Congratulations

503

Congratulations

Heartiest Congratulations

Heartiest Congratulations

From

Heartiest Congratulations.

HEARTIEST CONGRATULATIONS

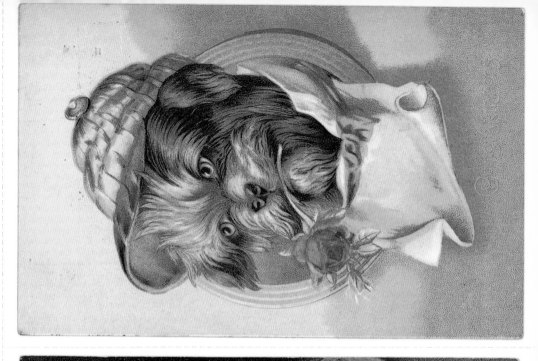

Heartiest Congratulations

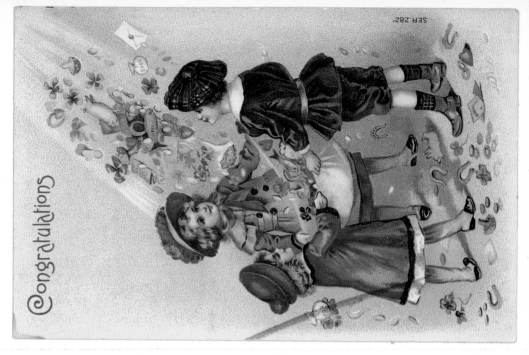

Congratulations

SER.282.

Accept
congratulations

SER. 667

Congratulations

Congratulations

1093.

From *The Old-Fashioned Congratulations Postcard Book* © by Sterling Publishing Co., Inc.

HEARTIEST
CONGRATULATIONS

SER. 25i

Congratulations

Congratulations

Heartiest Congratulations

Congratulations

Congratulations

Hearty Congratulation

Congratulations

Congratulations

Heartiest Congratulations

Send charming and beautifully designed cards throughout the year!

The Old-Fashioned Birthday Postcard Book
The Old-Fashioned Christmas Postcard Book
The Old-Fashioned Christmas for Kids Postcard Book
The Old-Fashioned Congratulations Postcard Book
The Old-Fashioned Get Well Postcard Book
The Old-Fashioned Happy Anniversary Postcard Book
The Old-Fashioned Holiday Postcard Book
The Old-Fashioned Love & Friendship Postcard Book
The Old-Fashioned Party Invitation Postcard Book
The Old-Fashioned Thank You Postcard Book
The Old-Fashioned Thinking of You Postcard Book

Filled with classic art from rare, turn-of-the-century originals, each book has 40 full-color, ready-to-mail postcards. They're a wonderful alternative to expensive commercial greeting cards. They're also a simple way to send thoughtful and tastefully designed cards throughout the year. Both friends and loved ones will cherish these unique examples of the cardmaker's art from the past.

 **A Sterling/Main Street Book**
Sterling Publishing Co., Inc.   New York